The Wit and Wisdom of Sheep Dogs

This is a STAR FIRE book

STAR FIRE BOOKS
Crabtree Hall, Crabtree Lane
Fulham, London SW6 6TY
United Kingdom

www.star-fire.co.uk

First published 2008

08 10 12 11 09

1 3 5 7 9 10 8 6 4 2

Star Fire is part of The Foundry Creative Media Company Limited

The CIP record for this book is available from the British Library.

ISBN: 978 1 84786 196 2

Printed in China

Thanks to: Chelsea Edwards and Nick Wells

Picture Credits

Images courtesy of: page 7 © Anna Dickie/Shutterstock; 8 © Sarah Johnson/Shutterstock;
11 © Alan Wesley/Shutterstock; 13, 15, 51, 52 © Iztok Noc/Shutterstock; 17, 19,
72 © Petspicture/Shutterstock; 20 © Mark Bond/Shutterstock; 23 © Donna Heatfield/
Shutterstock; 24, 42, 59 © Pontus Edenberg/Shutterstock; 27 © Brian Stewart-Coxon/Fotolia;
28 © Eline Spek/iStockphoto; 31 © Kati Molin/Fotolia; 4, 32 © Louise Wilkie/Fotolia; 35, 45, 55
© Kevin McGrath/Fotolia; 37 © Peter Guess/Shutterstock; 1, 3, 39, 41, 71 © Andi Taranczuk/
Fotolia; 47 © PeteG/Fotolia; 49 © Andrea Butterworth/Fotolia; 56 © Sally Wallis/iStockphoto;
61, 65 © Cerae/Fotolia; 63 © Tommy Martin/iStockphoto; 66 © Andris Piebalgs/Fotolia;
69 © k9stock/Fotolia

The Wit and Wisdom of Sheep Dogs

Ulysses Brave

Foreword

Sheep dogs are the heroes of the countryside.
Leaping, racing, herding and looking
important requires the development of
specialist skills and years of practise. Packed
with common sense and observation this
little book will provide a treasure trove
of such straightforward advice to owners
and sheep dogs alike.

Ulysses Brave

Think of ball games as part of your work-life balance.

Be relaxed in front of competition,
but always be alert.

A trip to the hairdresser can be relied on to cheer you up.

Looking cute, but deadly is an art form which requires constant practise.

Dummying, dodging and wind resistance should be core tasks in your training plans.

A simple Zen exercise each morning will keep you awake and alert throughout the day.

Braces are more common
now than when we were young,
sucking the wrong sweets and
dissolving our teeth before
we knew better.

Sometimes it's better to wait for the wind to die down before attempting to move forward.

Alternative methods of transport can be useful when recovering from illness.

*If you're going to leap
in, just do it!*

Sleeping rough? Late night?
Just look confident, no-one
will know!

Throw some shapes as an early morning exercise. Then go home for a well-deserved rest.

Sometimes life presents a simple problem. Perhaps running at it very hard could work?

Carefree and happy? Depends on your perspective – chasing sheep, or being chased by bears!

*Staying alert is difficult
when suffering from a
stomach bug.*

*Practise your sneaking
and tracking techniques on
compliant everyday objects.*

Developing nasal strength
is essential to the excellent
function of your work.

Try and pick your targets carefully. If they're bigger than you, make sure they can't get you back.

Leaping in once is probably enough to prove your manhood. Repeated dips demonstrate something else.

Try to choose appropriate hiding places.

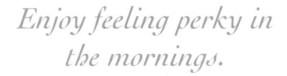

*Enjoy feeling perky in
the mornings.*

Don't forget to groom for that important meeting.

Cute displays of
uncharacteristic behaviour
only work if the audience
includes a genetic scientist.

I've got a headache!

Sunning yourself in the garden is fine, but only if it's your own.

Have some dignity in your practise.

Always test the
temperature
before leaping in.

*Being unbearably cute is
no excuse for being
unbearably cute...*

Have a rest by all means,
but don't take all day!

If you're late, try to find the quickest route to your destination.

Making friends is easy, if you're feeling safe!

Striking a sculptural pose works well when asked a difficult question. A lifelong technique, it will take years of practise to perfect.

French kissing requires
enthusiastic practise
with the tongue.

Come back soon!